S0-AWG-478

Sing, Sign, & Learn

Learn American Sign Language & Build Basic Skills
While Singing 25 Delightful Songs

Come

Tip-Toe

Quiet

I/Me

by Sherrill B. Flora

illustrated by Julie Anderson

Coat

Smile

Sing

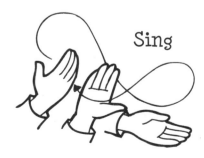

Purple

Key Education
An imprint of Carson-Dellosa Publishing, LLC
Greensboro, North Carolina

keyeducationpublishing.com

CONGRATULATIONS ON YOUR PURCHASE OF A KEY EDUCATION PRODUCT!

The editors at Key Education are former teachers who bring experience, enthusiasm, and quality to each and every product. Thousands of teachers have looked to the staff at Key Education for new and innovative resources to make their work more enjoyable and rewarding. We are committed to developing educational materials that will assist teachers in building a strong and developmentally appropriate curriculum for young children.

PLAN FOR GREAT TEACHING EXPERIENCES WHEN YOU USE EDUCATIONAL MATERIALS FROM KEY EDUCATION PUBLISHING

Credits

Authors: Sherrill B. Flora
Inside Illustrations: Julie Anderson
Editors: Claude Chalk
Page Design & Layout: Key Education Staff
Cover Design & Production: Annette Hollister-Papp
Cover Photo Credit: © Shutterstock

References

Capirci, O., Cattani, A., Rossinni P., Volterra, V. (1998). "Teaching sign language to hearing children as a possible factor in cognitive enhancement." Journal of Deaf Studies and Deaf Education, 3:2 Spring, 135–142.

Daniels, M. (1993). "ASL as a possible factor in the acquisition of English for hearing children." Sign Language Studies, 78, 23–29.

Daniels, M. (2001). *Dancing with words: signing for hearing children's literacy.* Westport, Connecticut: Bergin and Garvey.

Daniels, M. (1994). "The effect of sign language on hearing children's language development." Communication Education, 43:4, 291–298.

Key Education

An imprint of Carson-Dellosa Publishing, LLC
PO Box 35665
Greensboro, NC 27425 USA
www.keyeducationpublishing.com

ISBN 978-1-602680-80-7
02-147138091

Table of Contents

Introduction

Benefits of Teaching American Sign Language

Current research has documented that when young children are ready to learn how to read, that learning sign language can strengthen and increase oral language and literacy skills. In two different studies (Capirci, 1998), ASL was taught in context to children during their first- and second-grade years. The children in both studies who received the instruction scored higher on tests in visual discrimination and spatial memory than did the groups of children who did not receive any signing instruction. Other studies (Daniels, 1994) have consistently found that young hearing children who learn ASL in a school context demonstrate a greater understanding of English vocabulary and achieve higher scores on the Peabody Picture Vocabulary Test (PPVT) than their peers who did not receive any instruction.

We have also learned a great deal about multiple intelligences from Howard Gardner–and the importance of understanding and identifying the wide variety of individual learning styles as well as the importance of multisensory teaching. Sign language and music involves seeing, hearing, and movement–the perfect combination of all the ways that young children love to learn. Using the multisensory approaches of sign language, children are able to use both sides of the brain, thus creating multiple pathways which can strengthen memory and build connections for further learning.

Understanding the Different Varieties of Sign Language

American Sign Language (**ASL**) is an actual language – a visual language – that can be translated just like Spanish. It has its own syntax and grammar and does not follow exactly how English is spoken.

Signed Exact English (**SEE**) is a manually coded form of English that uses many ASL signs, but also incorporates special signs or inflections that allow English to be signed exactly as it is spoken.

Pidgin Signed English (**PSE**) is a combination of **ASL** and **English**. With PSE, people will use ASL signs for most of the vocabulary words in a sentence and follow English word order, but will not sign words that do not give essential knowledge or information to the sentence. For example, when using PSE, the sentence "Do you want to play?" would be signed as "You want play?"

Sing, Sign, & Learn uses PSE, the combination of ASL vocabulary signs and English. **When singing a song, sing all the words. When signing a song, sign only the words that are crucial for understanding the meaning of the song.** The words in parentheses will be sung, but they will not be signed.

FINGER NAMES AND HAND POSITIONS

The following chart illustrates the finger names and hand positions (handshapes) routinely used in American Sign Language (ASL). The chart also provides in **BOLD type** the names used in the sign descriptions featured in this book. The terms have been changed because the author has found, for example, that the term "open hand" instead of "'5' handshape" is easier for young children to understand and remember. The ASL terms have also been included for your personal reference.

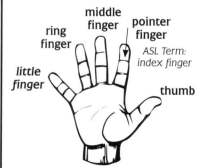

ring finger, **middle finger**, **pointer finger** (ASL Term: *index finger*), **little finger**, **thumb**

open hand
ASL Term: "5" handshape

flat hand
ASL Term: open handshape or flat "B"

claw hand
ASL Term: curved "5"

closed hand or fist
ASL Term: "A" handshape

OTHER NECESSARY VOCABULARY: In order for young children to successfully learn how to make hand signs they need to understand the following vocabulary: *forward, backward, up, down, front, back,* and *palm*. It is recommended that the teacher take some time to teach these words before beginning sign language instruction.

List of Signs

alphabet signs A–Z
all
always
and
another
arm
around
awake
ball
beautiful
bed
begin
bend
berries
big/large
bird
bite
black
blocks
blue
boot
brown
bump
bunny/rabbit
call
catch
chew
chicken
cleanup
closed/shut
coat
color
come
cow
dance
day
do
done/finish
don't
down
duck
eat
elbow

everyone
excited
excuse me
face
farm
favorite
fish
fly
foot
forget
friend
frog
fun
game
glove
go
good
good-bye
green
gulp
happy
hat
he/she
head
hello
help
here
higher
his/hers
hold
home
how
hurry
I
jelly
jump
kitten/cat
know
left
let
like (fond of)
like (same)
line

line up
listen
little
long
look
love
mad
magic
man
manners
many
me
mess
monkey
morning
mother
mouse
my
name
napkin
no one
not
number signs 1–10
off
old
on
orange (color)
our
out
outside
peanut butter
phone
pick
pig
pink
play
please
police
pony/horse
pouring
puppy/dog
purple
put

put on
quiet
rain
rainbow
red
remember
right
room
row
run
sad
said
sandwich
say
scared
school
see
she/he
shout
show
sight
sing
sit
sleep
slow
smash
smile
snoring
sorry
special
spread
spin
stack
stand
swim
swing
table
tail
take
take turns
thank-you
there
they/them

throw
time
tip-toe
tired
today
trees
turn
up
very
walk
want
watch
we
wear
what
when
where
white
who
word
work
yellow
yes
you
your
zoo

SONG 1

The Alphabet Song

Use this song to teach children how to fingerspell the letters of the alphabet. Teach one or two letters at a time until the children are able to accurately make the alphabet signs.

a

b

c

d

e

f

g

h

i

j

k

l

m

n

o

p

q

r

s

t u v w

 x

 y

and
Open hand moves in front of chest while fingers pull together.

and

 z

I
Point to yourself using the right pointer finger.

(Now) I

know
Fingertips of a flat hand touches the temple.

know

my
Place the palm of the right hand flat on the chest.

my

A B Cs

time
The right pointer finger taps the left wrist several times on the spot where one would wear a watch.

(next) time

please
The hand is open and flat and moves in a circular motion on the chest.

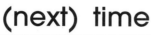

please

sing
The right hand is open and waves back and forth above the left arm, as if conducting a choir.

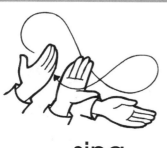

sing

me
Point to yourself using the right pointer finger.

(with) me.

SONG 2

What's Your Name?

What's Your Name?
(Sung to: "Where is Thumbkin?")

What is your name? What is your name?

My name's _____.

My name's _____.

You and I can be friends.

Very, very, good friends.

I like you. I like you.

what
The right pointer finger passes over the palm of the left hand.

your
The flat right hand, palm facing out and fingers together, moves forward.

name
Both hands make the letter "U" and then cross each other to form an "X."

What   (is)   your   name?

what
The right pointer finger passes over the palm of the left hand.

your
The flat right hand, palm facing out and fingers together, moves forward.

name
Both hands make the letter "U" and then cross each other to form an "X."

What   (is)   your   name?

my
Place the palm of the right hand flat on the chest.

name
Both hands make the letter "U" and then cross each other to form an "X."

My

name's

(fingerspell name)
_____ .

my
Place the palm of the right hand flat on the chest.

name
Both hands make the letter "U" and then cross each other to form an "X."

My

name's

(fingerspell name) .
_____

you
The pointer finger is pointed straight ahead. This is a natural gesture for indicating a person.

me
Point to yourself using the right pointer finger.

friends
The pointer fingers lock together, and then change positions and lock together in the opposite direction.

You   (and)   I   (can   be)   friends.

very
Make a "V" with both hands touching in front of chest and then move apart until hands are in front of the shoulders.

good
The flat hand moves from touching the mouth to being in front of the body, as if something was tasted.

friends
The pointer fingers lock together, and then change positions and lock together in the opposite direction.

Very,   very,   good   friends.

I
Point to yourself using the right pointer finger.

like
The thumb and pointer finger pinch together by the chest and move outward as if pulling the heart.

you
The pointer finger is pointed straight ahead. This is a natural gesture for indicating a person.

I   like   you.   *(Sing line twice.)*

SONG 3 Where is . . . ?

Where is . . . ?
(Sung to: "This Old Man")

Where is *(child's name)*?   Where is *(he/she)*?
(Child's name) please come sit by me.
With a great big happy smile, let the day begin.
(Child's name) is one of our good friends.

where
The pointer finger is held up and shaken side to side.

(sing or fingerspell name)

Where   **(is)**   **(child's name)?**

where
The pointer finger is held up and shaken side to side.

he/she
Pointer finger points to the side or to the person.

Where   **(is)**   **he/she?**

(sing or fingerspell name)

please
The hand is open and flat and moves in a circular motion on the chest.

come
Both pointer fingers beckon, or move towards the body, to indicate the concept of come.

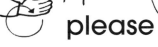

(Child's name)   **please**   **come**

sit
The right pointer and middle fingers are draped over the same two fingers on the left hand. The fingers look like they are sitting.

me
Point to yourself using the right pointer finger.

sit (by) me.

big
Both hands sign the letter "L." Then, with hands in front and palms facing each other, move hands away from each other showing that something is big.

happy
The open hand, with the palm facing the body, pats the heart in a circular motion.

smile
Person really smiles and places both hands in a "C" position on each side of the mouth. Then, pull and pinch the fingers back and upward past each cheek in the shape of a smile.

(With a great) big   happy   smile,

let
"L" shaped hands are pointing down and then move to point straight ahead.

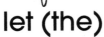

day
Place the left arm parallel to the ground, palm down. Then, with the right hand in a "D" shape, rest the right elbow on the left hand and move the right hand to the left elbow.

begin
The pointer finger twists between the fingers of the other hand and pretend to use a key to turn on a car.

let (the)   day   begin.

our
A flat curved hand is moved from one shoulder to the other shoulder.

(sing or fingerspell name)

good
The flat hand moves from touching the mouth to being in front of the body, as if something was tasted.

friends
The pointer fingers lock together, and then change positions and lock together in the opposite direction.

(child's name) (is one of) our   good   friends.

SONG 4

It's Time to Cleanup

It's Time to Cleanup
(Sung to: "A Hunting We Will Go")

It's time to cleanup our room.

It's time to cleanup our room.

We all say "yes," and cleanup our mess.

It's time to cleanup our room.

time
The right pointer finger taps the left wrist several times on the spot where one would wear a watch.

cleanup
With the hands flat, one hand wipes off the other hand.

our
A flat curved hand is moved from one shoulder to the other shoulder.

room
Flat hands, with fingers facing forward. Then, move flat hands so one is close to the chest and the other is in front of the chest, as if making the four walls of a room.

(It's) time   **(to) cleanup**   **our**   **room.**

time
The right pointer finger taps the left wrist several times on the spot where one would wear a watch.

cleanup
With the hands flat, one hand wipes off the other hand.

our
A flat curved hand is moved from one shoulder to the other shoulder.

room
Flat hands, with fingers facing forward. Then, move flat hands so one is close to the chest and the other is in front of the chest, as if making the four walls of a room.

(It's) time   **(to) cleanup**   **our**   **room.**

we
The pointer finger moves from one shoulder to the other shoulder.

We (all)

say
The pointer finger taps the chin twice.

say

yes
The hand makes the letter "S" and then moves up and down like a head nodding.

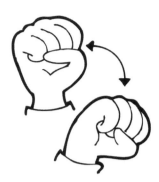

"yes,"

cleanup
With the hands flat, one hand wipes off the other hand.

(and) cleanup

our
A flat curved hand is moved from one shoulder to the other shoulder.

our

mess
Hold hands in a curved shape with the right hand over the left hand. Then twist hands back and forth as if turning something upside down and making a mess.

mess.

time
The right pointer finger taps the left wrist several times on the spot where one would wear a watch.

(It's) time

cleanup
With the hands flat, one hand wipes off the other hand.

(to) cleanup

our
A flat curved hand is moved from one shoulder to the other shoulder.

our

room
Flat hands, with fingers facing forward. Then, move flat hands so one is close to the chest and the other is in front of the chest, as if making the four walls of a room.

room.

SONG 5 Let's Line Up

Let's Line Up
(Sung to: "Three Blind Mice")

Please line up. Please line up.
All in a row. All in a row.
We all line up in a quiet row.
Not in a hurry and we walk slow.
Once in our line, we're ready to go.
Please line up. Please line up.

please
The hand is open and flat and moves in a circular motion on the chest.

Please

line up
Both hands make the letter "B" with the fingers apart and the left hand in front of the right. Then the hands are pulled apart to represent a line of people.

line up.

(Sing line twice.)

all
The hand moves in a circle and then ends up in the palm of the other hand. Shows that everything (all) has been included.

All (in a)

row/line
The fingertips of the little fingers touch and then pull apart.

row.

(Sing line twice.)

we
The pointer finger moves from one shoulder to the other shoulder.

We (all)

line up
Both hands make the letter "B" with the fingers apart and the left hand in front of the right. Then the hands are pulled apart to represent a line of people.

line up

quiet
Both pointer fingers are in front of the mouth, as if saying "shhh." Then, at the same time, open both hands while moving downward.

(in a) quiet

row/line
The fingertips of the little fingers touch and then pull apart.

row.

not
The right thumb is held under the chin and then pulled forward.

hurry
Move hands in "H" shapes quickly up and down in front of the body.

Not (in a)   hurry

we
The pointer finger moves from one shoulder to the other shoulder.

walk
With both hands flat, fingers pointing forward and held in front of the chest, the hands sway back and forth as if they are walking.

slow
One flat hand, palm facing the ground, is still. The other flat hand "slowly" strokes the still hand.

(and) we   walk   slow.

our
A flat curved hand is moved from one shoulder to the other shoulder.

line/row
The fingertips of the little fingers touch and then pull apart.

go
Both pointer fingers move in an arch and point away from the body.

(Once in) our line, (we're ready to) go.

please
The hand is open and flat and moves in a circular motion on the chest.

line up
Both hands make the letter "B" with the fingers apart and the left hand in front of the right. Then the hands are pulled apart to represent a line of people.

Please   line up.   *(Sing line twice.)*

SONG 6 Hello and Good-bye Song

Hello and Good-Bye Song
(Sung to: "Jimmy Crack Corn")

Oh, look at me and say "hello."

Oh, look at me and say "hello."

Oh, look at me and say "hello."

Good morning my good friends.

(verse 2)
Oh, look at me and wave "good-bye."

The school day is all done.

look
The hand makes the letter "V," palm side of the hand toward the body. The hand touches the eyes and then swings back out so the fingers are pointing forward.

me
Point to yourself using the right pointer finger.

say
The pointer finger taps the chin twice.

hello
The open hand waves back and forth.

(Oh,) look   **(at) me**   **(and) say**   **"hello."**

look
The hand makes the letter "V," palm side of the hand toward the body. The hand touches the eyes and then swings back out so the fingers are pointing forward.

me
Point to yourself using the right pointer finger.

say
The pointer finger taps the chin twice.

hello
The open hand waves back and forth.

(Oh,) look   **(at) me**   **(and) say**   **"hello."**

look
The hand makes the letter "V," palm side of the hand toward the body. The hand touches the eyes and then swings back out so the fingers are pointing forward.

me
Point to yourself using the right pointer finger.

say
The pointer finger taps the chin twice.

hello
The hand waves back and forth.

(Oh,) look (at) me (and) say "hello."

good
The flat hand moves from touching the mouth to being in front of the body, as if something was tasted.

morning
Right arm bends at the elbow with the flat right hand's palm facing the chest. The left hand is placed on the inside of the right bent elbow. The right flat hand then moves like the the sun rising.

good
The flat hand moves from touching the mouth to being in front of the body, as if something was tasted.

friends
The pointer fingers lock together, and then change positions and lock together in the opposite direction.

my
Place the palm of the right hand flat on the chest.

Good morning my good friends.

(Verse 2)

look
The hand makes the letter "V," palm side of the hand toward the body. The hand touches the eyes and then swings back out so the fingers are pointing forward.

me
Point to yourself using the right pointer finger.

good-bye
The hand waves back and forth.

(Sing line 3 times.)

(Oh,) look (at) me (and wave) "good-bye."

school
The right flat hand claps twice (straight up and down) on the flat left palm. (The teacher clapping twice to get attention.)

day
Place the left arm parallel to the ground, palm down. Then, with the right hand in a "D" shape, rest the right elbow on the left hand and move the right hand to the left elbow.

done
Both hands are open with palms facing the chest, fingers pointing up. Then, quickly flip the hands over ending with the palms down and fingers pointing forward.

(The) school day (is all) done.

KE-804084 © Key Education — - 17 - — *Sing, Sign, & Learn!*

SONG 7 Play Outside

Play Outside
(Sung to: "London Bridge")

Now, its time to play outside.

Play outside. Play outside.

Now, its time to play outside.

(Verse 1) Put on your <u>coat</u>.

(Verse 2)
Put on your <u>boots</u>.

(Verse 3)
Put on your <u>hat</u>.

(Verse 4)
Put on your <u>gloves</u>.

(The first three lines are the same in each verse.)

time
The right pointer finger taps the left wrist several times on the spot where one would wear a watch.

play
Both hands make the letter "Y" and twist back and forth at the same time.

outside
The left hand lightly grabs the right hand. The right hand is then pulled up and out.

(Now, its) time   (to) play   outside.

play
Both hands make the letter "Y" and twist back and forth at the same time.

outside
The left hand lightly grabs the right hand and then pulls it up and out.

play
Both hands make the letter "Y" and twist back and forth at the same time.

outside
The left hand lightly grabs the right hand. The right hand is then pulled up and out.

Play   outside.   Play   outside.

time
The right pointer finger taps the left wrist several times on the spot where one would wear a watch.

play
Both hands make the letter "Y" and twist back and forth at the same time.

outside
The left hand lightly grabs the right hand. The right hand is then pulled up and out.

(Now, its) time   (to) play   outside.

put on
With open hands, brush the thumbs along each side of the chest

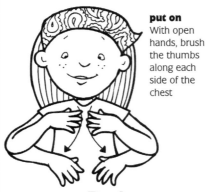

your
The flat right hand, palm facing out and fingers together, moves forward.

coat
Both hands make the letter "A" and then, as if holding the sides of a coat, pull down from the collar to the waist.

(Verse 1) Put on   your   coat.

---

put on
With open hands, brush the thumbs along each side of the chest

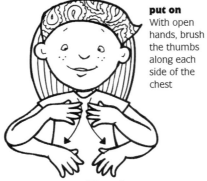

your
The flat right hand, palm facing out and fingers together, moves forward.

boots
Both hands in the "S" shape tap together (sign for shoe), Then, the right flat hand touches the left elbow–showing that it is a "tall" shoe/boot.

(Verse 2) Put on   your   boots.

---

put on
With open hands, brush the thumbs along each side of the chest

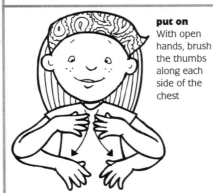

your
The flat right hand, palm facing out and fingers together, moves forward.

hat
The open right hand taps the top of the head twice.

(Verse 3) Put on   your   hat.

---

put on
With open hands, brush the thumbs along each side of the chest

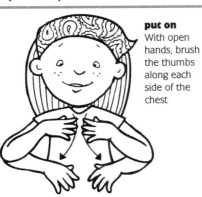

your
The flat right hand, palm facing out and fingers together, moves forward.

gloves
With open hands, the right hand moves up the back of the left hand (from fingertips to the wrist) and then the left hand does the same thing to the right hand. (Just like pulling a glove on each hand.)

(Verse 4) Put on   your   gloves.

SONG 4 — Let's Go

Let's Go
(Sung to: "Are You Sleeping?")

(Verse 1) Let's go walking. Let's go walking.

Here we go. Here we go.

We love to go walking.

Walking — Walking — Walking.

Walking fun. Walking fun.

(Verse 2) Let's go running.   (Verse 4) Let's go dancing.

(Verse 3) Let's go jumping.   (Verse 5) Let's go tip-toeing.

let
"L" shaped hands are pointing down and then move to point straight ahead.

Let's

go
Both pointer fingers move in an arch and point away from the body.

go

walk
With both hands flat, fingers pointing forward and held in front of the chest, the hands sway back and forth as if they are walking.

walking.

let
"L" shaped hands are pointing down and then move to point straight ahead.

Let's

go
Both pointer fingers move in an arch and point away from the body.

go

walk
With both hands flat, fingers pointing forward and held in front of the chest, the hands sway back and forth as if they are walking.

walking.

here
Both hands are held palms up and make small circles in front of the chest.

we
The pointer finger moves from one shoulder to the other shoulder.

go
Both pointer fingers move in an arch and point away from the body.

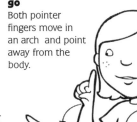

Here   we   go. *(Sing line twice.)*

we
The pointer finger moves from one shoulder to the other shoulder.

love
Fists cross at the wrist and then lay upon the chest.

go
Both pointer fingers move in an arch and point away from the body.

walk
With both hands flat, fingers pointing forward and held in front of the chest, the hands sway back and forth as if they are walking.

We   love   (to) go   walking.

walk
With both hands flat, fingers pointing forward and held in front of the chest, the hands sway back and forth as if they are walking.

walk
With both hands flat, fingers pointing forward and held in front of the chest, the hands sway back and forth as if they are walking.

walk
With both hands flat, fingers pointing forward and held in front of the chest, the hands sway back and forth as if they are walking.

Walking — Walking — Walking

walk
With both hands flat, fingers pointing forward and held in front of the chest, the hands sway back and forth as if they are walking.

fun
Touch nose with the pointer and middle fingers. Then move those fingers down to touch the other pointer and middle fingers.

walk
With both hands flat, fingers pointing forward and held in front of the chest, the hands sway back and forth as if they are walking.

fun
Touch nose with the pointer and middle fingers. Then move those fingers down to touch the other pointer and middle fingers.

Walking   fun.   Walking   fun.

Additional Verses for "Let's Go"

run
Each hand looks like a slightly bent letter "L." The pointer finger of one hand pulls on the thumb of the other hand as both hands move forward.

While the hands move forward the extended thumb and pointer finger are wiggled.

2. Running Verse
"Let's go running."

jump
The right hand is held in an upside down "V" position and jumps up and down on the palm of the left hand.

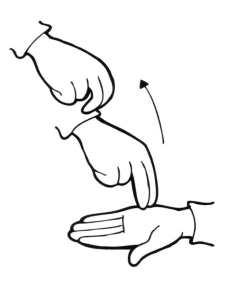

3. Jumping Verse
"Let's go jumping."

dance
The right hand is held in an upside down "V" and then dances on the palm of the left hand.

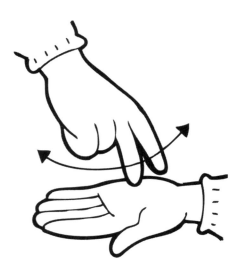

4. Dancing Verse
"Let's go dancing."

tip-toe
Pointer fingers are both pointing down and are alternating moving up and down as if tip-toeing.

5. Tip-Toeing Verse
"Let's go tip-toeing."

SONG 9 Listen & Do

Listen & Do
(Sung to: "Farmer in the Dell")

Oh, listen and stand up.
Oh, listen and sit down.
Stand up everyone.
And, please spin around. *(Yell "now sit down.")*

listen The hand is cupped behind the ear – implying that the ears should listen.

(Oh,) listen

stand up The right hand is held in an upside down "V" and stands on the palm of the left hand.

(and) stand up.

listen The hand is cupped behind the ear – implying that the ears should listen.

(Oh,) listen

sit The right pointer and middle fingers are draped over the same two fingers on the left hand. The fingers look like they are sitting.

(and) sit down.

stand up The right hand is held in an upside down "V" and stands on the palm of the left hand.

Stand up

everyone First, make the sign for "each:" Both fists make the "thumbs up" sign. Then the right hand knuckles brush down against the left hand knuckles. End with making the sign ofr "one."

everyone.

please The hand is open and flat and moves in a circular motion on the chest.

(And,) please

spin around Move pointer finger, pointing down in a circle around the left pointer finger that is pointing up.

spin around.

SONG 10 Following Directions

Following Directions
(Sung to: "A Hunting We Will Go")

Verse 1:
Oh, put your left foot out.
Oh, put your left foot out.
Hold it out and give a shout.
Oh, put your left foot out.

Verse 2:
Oh, bend your elbow down.
Oh, bend your elbow down.
Bend it down and spin around.
Oh, bend your elbow down.

(In verse 1, the word "right" can be substituted for the word "left.")

right
Right hand makes the letter "R" and then moves it to the right.

Verse 3:
Oh, turn your head—look down.
Oh, turn your head—look down.
Turn your head is what I said.
Oh, turn your head—look down

---

put
Both hands make the letter "O" with palms down. Then move hands at the same time up and forward as if putting something away.

left
Right hand makes letter "L" and moves from the right to the left across the chest.

foot
Point to foot.

out
Left hand holds the right hand, then the right hand pulls "out" of the left hand.

 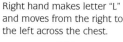 

(Verse 1)
(Oh,) put (your)   **left**   **foot**   **out.**

---

put
Both hands make the letter "O" with palms down. Then move hands at the same time up and forward as if putting something away

left
Right hand makes letter "L" and moves from the right to the left across the chest.

foot
Point to foot.

out
Left hand holds the right hand, then the right hand pulls "out" of the left hand.

(Oh,) put (your)   **left**   **foot**   **out.**

hold
With hands in fists, one hand is on top of the other hand as if holding something.

out
Left hand holds the right hand, then the right hand pulls "out" of the left hand.

shout
Close hand like a megaphone around the mouth and then move hand up and forward as if sound is being thrown forward.

Hold (it)   out (and give a)   shout.

put
Both hands make the letter ")" with palms down. Then move hands at the same time up and forward as if putting something away.

left
Right hand makes letter "L" and moves from the right to the left across the chest.

foot
Point to foot.

out
Left hand holds the right hand, then the right hand pulls "out" of the left hand.

(Oh,) put (your)   left   foot   out.

(Verse 2)

bend
Finger tips touch and then the right hand fingers bend the left hand fingers down until both palms are facing down and hands are bent.

your
The flat right hand, palm facing out and fingers together, moves forward.

elbow
Tap elbow with the pointer finger.

down
Pointer finger points down.

(Oh,) bend   your   elbow   down.

bend
Finger tips touch and then the right hand fingers bend the left hand fingers down until both palms are facing down and hands are bent.

your
The flat right hand, palm facing out and fingers together, moves forward.

elbow
Tap elbow with the pointer finger.

down
Pointer finger points down.

(Oh,) bend   your   elbow   down.

bend
Finger tips touch and then the right hand fingers bend the left hand fingers down until both palms are facing down and hands are bent.

down
Pointer finger points down in front of the body.

spin around
Move pointer finger, pointing down in a circle around the left pointer finger that is pointing up.

Bend (it)   down (and)   spin around.

bend
Finger tips touch and then the right hand fingers bend the left hand fingers down until both palms are facing down and hands are bent.

your
The flat right hand, palm facing out and fingers together, moves forward.

elbow
Tap elbow with the pointer finger.

down
Pointer finger points down.

(Oh,) bend   your   elbow   down.

(Verse 3)

turn
Hold hands in fists and place right hand on top of the left hand and twist.

your
The flat right hand, palm facing out and fingers together, moves forward.

head
Place fingertips on the right temple and then move them along the cheek to the jaw bone.

look
The hand makes the letter "V," palm side toward the body.

Then touch the eyes and swing back out so the fingers are pointing forward.

down
Pointer finger points down.

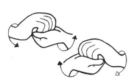 

(Oh,) turn   your   head — look   down.

---

turn
Hold hands in fists and place right hand on top of the left hand and twist.

your
The flat right hand, palm facing out and fingers together, moves forward.

head
Place fingertips on the right temple and then move them along the cheek to the jaw bone.

look
The hand makes the letter "V," palm side toward the body.

Then touch the eyes and swing back out so the fingers are pointing forward.

down
Pointer finger points down.

(Oh,) turn   your   head — look   down.

---

turn
Hold hands in fists and place right hand on top of the left hand and twist.

your
The flat right hand, palm facing out and fingers together, moves forward.

head
Place fingertips on the right temple and then move them along the cheek to the jaw bone.

I
Point to yourself using the right pointer finger

said
Touch lips with the pointer finger as if saying "shhh" and then move hand up and away.

Turn   your   head   (is what) I   said.

---

turn
Hold hands in fists and place right hand on top of the left hand and twist.

your
The flat right hand, palm facing out and fingers together, moves forward.

head
Place fingertips on the right temple and then move them along the cheek to the jaw bone.

look
The hand makes the letter "V," palm side toward the body.

Then touch the eyes and swing back out so the fingers are pointing forward.

down
Pointer finger points down.

(Oh,) turn   your   head — look   down.

Who is Wearing?

(Color Songs)

Who is Wearing?
(Sung to: "The Muffin Man")

Who is wearing *(color)* today?
(Color) today? *(Color)* today?
Who is wearing *(color)* today?
(He/she) is wearing *(color)*.

(Point to a child wearing that color.)

(See pages 28 and 29 for the color signs.)

---

who
The thumb touches the chin and the pointer finger bends several times by the mouth.

wear
Make a "U" shape with fingers pointing upward and palm facing forward. Move hand in a circular motion in front of the right side of the body twice.

today
Both hands make a "Y" so that the fingers are facing the body. Move both "Y" hands slightly back and forth.

Who   (is)   wearing   *(sign a color)*   today?

---

today
Both hands make a "Y" so that the fingers are facing the body. Move both "Y" hands slightly back and forth.

today
Both hands make a "Y" so that the fingers are facing the body. Move both "Y" hands slightly back and forth.

***(sign a color)* today?   *(sign a color)* today?**

who
The thumb touches the chin and the pointer finger bends several times by the mouth.

wear
Make a "U" shape with fingers pointing upward and palm facing forward. Move hand in a circular motion in front of the right side of the body twice.

today
Both hands make a "Y" so that the fingers are facing the body. Move both "Y" hands slightly back and forth.

Who (is) wearing *(sign a color)* today?

---

he/she
Pointer finger points to the side or to the person.

wear
Make a "U" shape with fingers pointing upward and palm facing forward. Move hand in a circular motion in front of the right side of the body twice.

He (or) She (is) wearing *(sign a color)*.

Color Signs for "Who is Wearing?"

red
The pointer finger strokes the lips in an up and down motion. (Lips are red.)

Sign for "red."

green
The hand makes the letter "G" and shakes back and forth.

Sign for "green."

yellow
The hand makes the letter "Y" and shakes back and forth.

Sign for "yellow."

blue
The hand makes the letter "B" and shakes back and forth.

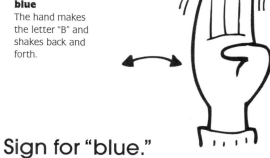

Sign for "blue."

purple
The hand makes the letter "P" and shakes back and forth.

Sign for "purple."

orange (color)
The open hand makes the letter "C" and is held at the mouth, then it squeezes as if squeezing an orange.

Sign for "orange."

pink
The hand makes the letter "P" and strokes the lips with the middle finger.

Sign for "pink."

white
The hand makes a claw and is placed on the chest, and then it is pulled straight out with the fingertips coming together.

Sign for "white."

black
The pointer finger draws a line across the forehead.

Sign for "black."

brown
The hand makes the letter "B" and slides down the side of the cheek.

Sign for "brown."

SONG 12 Rainbow Colors

Rainbow Colors
(Sung to: "I've Been Working on the Railroad")

Red, blue, yellow, green, and purple,
Orange, pink, black, and brown.
All the colors of the rainbow.
You can see them all around.
Don't forget my favorite color.
The color that's called white.
There are so many colors,
Oh, what a beautiful sight.

red
The pointer finger strokes the lips. (Lips are red.)

blue
The hand makes the letter "B" and shakes back and forth.

yellow
The hand makes the letter "Y" and shakes back and forth.

green
The hand makes the letter "G" and shakes back and forth.

purple
The hand makes the letter "P" and shakes back and forth.

Red,   blue,   yellow,   green, (and) purple,

orange
The open hand makes the letter "C" and is held at the mouth, then it squeezes as if squeezing an orange.

pink
The hand makes the letter "P" and strokes the lips with the middle finger.

black
The pointer finger draws a line across the forehead.

brown
The hand makes the letter "B" and slides down the side of the cheek.

Orange,   pink ,   black,   (and) brown.

all
The hand moves in a circle and then ends up in the palm of the other hand. Indicates "all" included.

color
Point the fingertips toward the mouth and wiggle them as the hand moves slightly forward.

rainbow
Make a "4" shape and then move the hand in an arch from the shoulder across the body (making the arch of a rainbow).

All (the)   colors   (of the) rainbow.

you
The pointer finger is pointed straight ahead. This is a natural gesture for indicating a person.

see
The hand makes the letter "V," palm side of the hand toward the body. The hand touches the eyes and then swings back out so the fingers are pointing forward.

all around
Move pointer finger, pointing down in a circle around the left pointer finger that is pointing up.

You (can)   see (them)   all around.

don't
Cross hands in front of chest and then swing down to the side of the body, as if saying, "don't."

forget
Fingertips wipe across the forehead as if you have forgotten something.

favorite
With open hand, middle finger touches chin twice.

color
Point the fingertips toward the mouth and wiggle them as the hand moves slightly forward.

Don't   forget   (my) favorite   color.

color
Point the fingertips toward the mouth and wiggle them as the hand moves slightly forward.

white
The hand makes a claw and is placed on the chest, and then it is pulled straight out with the fingertips coming together.

(The) color   (that's called)   white.

there
The right pointer is pointing forward in front of the right shoulder and moves forward as if pointing to "there."

many
Both hands make a fist in front of the chest. Then, quickly flick the fingers open twice.

color
Point the fingertips toward the mouth and wiggle them as the hand moves slightly forward.

There (are so)   many   colors.

what
The right pointer finger passes over the palm of the left hand.

beautiful
Right open hand circles the face, while closing the fingers to the thumb. Then move hand forward and quickly spread fingers open.

sight/picture
The right hand makes the letter "C" in front of the eye and then moves down to the open palm of the other hand.

(Oh,) what (a)   beautiful   sight.

SONG 13 Count the Animals

(Other verses found on pages 34 and 35.)

Count the Animals
(Sung to: "One Little, Two Little, Three Little. . .")

(Verse 1) One little, two little, three little kittens.
Four little, five little, six little kittens.
Seven little, eight little, nine little kittens.
Ten little kittens sleeping.

One

little
Flat hands move together, showing that something is little.

little,

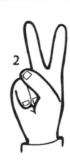

two

little
Flat hands move together, showing that something is little.

little,

three

little
Flat hands move together, showing that something is little.

little

kittens
On both hands, the pointer fingers and the thumbs are pinched together with the remaining fingers standing tall. Then the thumbs and pointer fingers are placed on either side of the nose, and then pinched and pulled as if pulling whiskers.

kittens.

Four

little
Flat hands move together, showing that something is little.

little,

five

little
Flat hands move together, showing that something is little.

little,

six

little

little
Flat hands move together, showing that something is little.

kittens.

kittens
On both hands, the pointer fingers and the thumbs are pinched together with the remaining fingers standing tall. Then the thumbs and pointer fingers are placed on either side of the nose, and then pinched and pulled as if pulling whiskers.

Seven

little,

little
Flat hands move together, showing that something is little.

eight

little,

little
Flat hands move together, showing that something is little.

nine

little

little
Flat hands move together, showing that something is little.

kittens.

kittens
On both hands, the pointer fingers and the thumbs are pinched together with the remaining fingers standing tall. Then the thumbs and pointer fingers are placed on either side of the nose, and then pinched and pulled as if pulling whiskers.

(Verse 10)

little
Flat hands move together, showing that something is little.

kittens
On both hands, the pointer fingers and the thumbs are pinched together with the remaining fingers standing tall. Then the thumbs and pointer fingers are placed on either side of the nose, and then pinched and pulled as if pulling whiskers.

sleep
Place flat hand against the cheek and pull down as if closing the eyes and going to sleep.

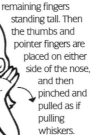

Ten

little

kittens

sleeping.

Additional Verses: Counting the Animals

Verse 2: . . . little birds flying.

bird
The pointer finger and thumb are held close to the mouth and then open and close like the beak of a bird.

Sign for "bird."

fly
Move arms as if flying like a bird.

Sign for "flying."

Verse 3: . . . little puppies playing.

puppy
Slap your knee with your hand and then snap your fingers, as if calling a dog.

Sign for "puppy."

play
Both hands make the letter "Y" and twist back and forth at the same time.

Sign for "playing."

Verse 4: . . . little fish swimming.

fish
The hands are open and make a swimming motion in front of the chest.

Sign for "fish."

swim
Flat hands, palms facing down, with fingertips touching in front of chest. Then, move hands apart to each side twice as if swimming.

Sign for "swimming."

Verse 5: . . . little mice running.

mouse
The pointer finger brushes past the nose twice.

Sign for "mice."

run
Each hand looks like a slightly bent letter "L." The pointer finger of one hand pulls on the thumb of the other hand as both hands move forward.

While the hands move forward the extended thumb and pointer finger are wiggled.

Sign for "running."

Verse 6: . . . little bunnies hopping.

bunny
Both hands make the letter "U" and are held backwards on either side of the head. Then the fingers hop up and down just like a rabbit's ears.

Sign for "bunny."

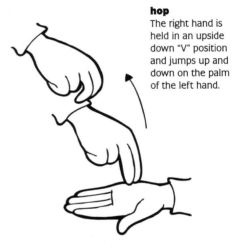

hop
The right hand is held in an upside down "V" position and jumps up and down on the palm of the left hand.

Sign for "hopping."

Verse 7: . . . little pigs eating.

pig
The hand makes the letter "B" and is placed palm down under the chin and the fingers flap up and down as one.

Sign for "pig."

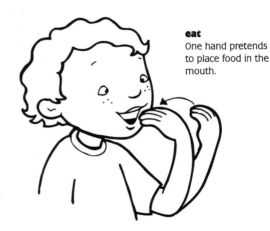

eat
One hand pretends to place food in the mouth.

Sign for "eating."

SONG 14 — There Was One Little Duck

There Was One Little Duck
(Sung to: "Ten in Bed")

Verse 1:
There was one little duck,
And he called to his friend,
"Let's go swim."
"Let's go swim."
So, the two jumped in and
Went for a swim.

Verse 2:
There were two little ducks,
And they called to their friend,
"Let's go swim."
"Let's go swim."
So, the three jumped in and
Went for a swim.

Verse 3: There were three little ducks . . . so, the four jumped in . . .
Verse 4: There were four little ducks . . . so, the five jumped in . . .
Verse 5: There were five little ducks . . . so, the six jumped in . . .
Verse 6: There were six little ducks . . . so, the seven jumped in . . .
Verse 7: There were seven little ducks . . . so, the eight jumped in . . .
Verse 8: There were eight little ducks . . . so, the nine jumped in . . .
Verse 9: There were nine little ducks . . . so, the ten jumped in . . .

Verse 10:
There were ten little ducks, and they swam all around.
Till their mother shouted, "Come home!" *(shout)*

(Verses 1-9)

(Number signs on page 38.)

there
The right pointer is pointing forward in front of the right shoulder and moves forward as if pointing to "there."

little
Flat hands move together, indicating that something is little.

duck
The pointer and middle fingers tap the thumb in front of the mouth to mimic the movement of a duck's bill.

There (was/were) (sign a number) little duck/s,

he
Pointer finger points to the side or to the person.

they
Move the right pointer finger back and forth in front of the body.

call
Place the hand on the side of the mouth as if really calling someone.

friend
The pointer fingers lock together, and then change positions and lock together in the opposite direction.

(And) he/they   called   (to his/their)   friend,

let
"L" shaped hands are pointing down and then move to point straight ahead.

go
Both pointer fingers move in an arch and point away from the body.

swim
Flat hands, palms facing down, with fingertips touching in front of chest. Then, move hands apart to each side twice as if swimming.

Let's   go   swim.   *(Sing line twice.)*

jump
The right hand is held in an upside down "V" position and jumps up and down on the palm of the left hand.

swim
Flat hands, palms facing down, with fingertips touching in front of chest. Then, move hands apart to each side twice as if swimming.

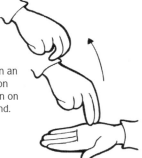 

(So, the) (sign a number) jumped in (and went for a) swim.

(Verse 10)

there
The right pointer is pointing forward in front of the right shoulder and moves forward as if pointing to "there."

little
Flat hands move together, indicating that something is little.

duck
The pointer and middle fingers tap the thumb in front of the mouth to mimic the movement of a duck's bill.

There (were)   ten   little   ducks,

they
Move the right pointer finger back and forth in front of the body.

swim
Flat hands, palms facing down, with fingertips touching in front of chest. Then, move hands apart to each side twice as if swimming.

around
Move pointer finger, pointing down in a circle around the left pointer finger that is pointing up.

(And) they   swam (all)   around.

mother
Touch the chin with the thumb of your open hand twice.

shout
Close hand like a megaphone around the mouth and then move hand up and forward as if sound is being thrown forward.

come
Both pointer fingers beckon, or move towards the body to indicate the concept of come.

home
Right hand makes an "O." Then fingers touch lips and moves to the cheek, indicating eat and sleep at home.

(Till their) mother   shouted, "Come home!"

1   2   3   4   5

6   7   8   9   10

SONG 15

Jump, Froggie, Jump!

(Counting Songs)

Jump, Froggie, Jump!
(Sung to: "Alice the Camel")

Verse 1: One little froggie jumped one time.
One little froggie jumped one time.
One little froggie jumped one time.
So, jump, froggie, jump!

Verse 2: Two little froggies jumped two times.
Verse 3: Three little froggies jumped three times.

(Continue with as many verses as you would like.)

little
Flat hands move together, indicating that something is little.

frog
Hold right hand forming the number "3" under the chin and make fingers open and close like a frog croaking.

jump
The right hand is held in an upside down "V" position and jumps up and down on the palm of the left hand.

(Number signs on page 38.)

time
The right pointer finger taps the left wrist several times on the spot where one would wear a watch.

(Sing line 3 times.)

(Sign a number) little froggie/s jumped (sign a number) time/s.

jump
The right hand is held in an upside down "V" position and jumps up and down on the palm of the left hand.

frog
Hold right hand forming the number "3" under the chin and make fingers open and close like a frog croaking.

jump
The right hand is held in an upside down "V" position and jumps up and down on the palm of the left hand.

(So,) jump,   **froggie/s,**   **jump!**

KE-804084 © Key Education ———— - 39 - ———— *Sing, Sign, & Learn!*

SONG
16

If You're Happy

(Self-Esteem/Feeling Songs)

If You're Happy
(Sung to: "If You're Happy and You Know It")

If you're happy and you know it, clap your hands.
If you're happy and you know it, clap your hands.
If you're happy and you know it,
Then your face will really show it.
If you're happy and you know it, clap your hands.

Verse 2: If you're mad and you know it,
stamp your feet.

Verse 3: If you're sad and you know it,
wipe your eyes.

Verse 4: If you're tired and you know it,
go to sleep.

Verse 5: If you're scared and you know it,
shiver all over.

you
The pointer finger is pointed straight ahead.

happy
The open hand, with the palm facing the body, pats the heart in a circular motion.

you
The pointer finger is pointed straight ahead.

know
Fingertips of a flat hand touches the temple.

(Clap your hands twice.)

(If) you're happy (and) you know (it), clap your hands.

you
The pointer finger is pointed straight ahead.

happy
The open hand, with the palm facing the body, pats the heart in a circular motion.

you
The pointer finger is pointed straight ahead.

know
Fingertips of a flat hand touches the temple.

(Clap your hands twice.)

(If) you're happy (and) you know (it), clap your hands.

you
The pointer finger is pointed straight ahead.

happy
The open hand, with the palm facing the body, pats the heart in a circular motion.

you
The pointer finger is pointed straight ahead.

know
Fingertips of a flat hand touches the temple.

(If) you're   happy (and)   you   know (it),

your
The flat right hand, palm facing out and fingers together, moves forward.

face
Right pointer finger draws a circle around the face.

show
The right pointer finger touches the palm of the left hand (close to the body.) Then, both hands move outward from the body.

(Then) your   face (will really)   show (it).

you
The pointer finger is pointed straight ahead.

happy
The open hand, with the palm facing the body, pats the heart in a circular motion.

you
The pointer finger is pointed straight ahead.

know
Fingertips of a flat hand touches the temple.

(Clap your hands twice.)

(If) you're happy (and) you know (it), clap your hands.

you
The pointer finger is pointed straight ahead.

mad
The hand is held like a claw in front of the face and strikes down or in a circular motion.

you
The pointer finger is pointed straight ahead.

know
Fingertips of a flat hand touches the temple.

(Stamp your feet twice.)

(If) you're mad (and) you know (it), stamp your feet.

you
The pointer finger is pointed straight ahead.

sad
With both hands open, fingers apart and slightly bent, palms facing toward the face – move the hands down at the same time to mouth level.

you
The pointer finger is pointed straight ahead.

know
Fingertips of a flat hand touches the temple.

(Wipe your eyes.)

(If) you're sad (and) you know (it), wipe your eyes.

you
The pointer finger is pointed straight ahead.

tired
The hands are placed on the chest and are moved downward along with the shoulders drooping to represent that someone does not have the strength to go on.

you
The pointer finger is pointed straight ahead.

know
Fingertips of a flat hand touches the temple.

(Pretend to fall asleep.)

(If) you're tired (and) you know (it), go to sleep.

you
The pointer finger is pointed straight ahead.

scared
Both hands in fists, move quickly in front of the body as if to protect it. The hands open when they are in front of the body.

you
The pointer finger is pointed straight ahead.

know
Fingertips of a flat hand touches the temple.

(Shiver and pretend to be scared.)

(If) you're scared (and) you know (it), shiver all over.

(Self-Esteem/Feeling Songs)

I am Special!

I am Special!
(Sung to: "Twinkle, Twinkle")

I am special. Look at me.

There is no one else like me.

Always trying to be good.

Doing work I know I should.

I am special. Look at me.

There is no one else like me.

I
Point to yourself using the right pointer finger.

special
Left hand grabs the pointer finger of the right hand and then pulls it up in front of the chest.

look
The hand makes the letter "V," palm side of the hand toward the body. The hand touches the eyes and then swings back out so the fingers are pointing forward.

me
Point to yourself using the right pointer finger.

I (am)   **special.**   **Look**   **(at) me.**

---

there
The pointer is pointing forward in front of the right shoulder and moves forward as if pointing to "there."

no one
Right hand makes the letter "O" and moves it from side to side a couple times.

like (same as)
Pointer fingers point forward and then move together showing that they are the same.

me
Point to yourself using the right pointer finger.

There (is)   **no one**   **(else)**   **like**   **me.**

---

always
The pointer finger points up and makes a circular motion in front of the chest.

good
The flat hand moves from touching the mouth to being in front of the body, as if something was tasted.

Always   (trying to be)   good.

do
Both hands make the letter "C." With palms down, move repeatedly from side to side.

work
Both hands make a fist and then the right wrist taps the back of the left wrist twice.

I
Point to yourself using the right pointer finger.

know
Fingertips of a flat hand touches the temple.

Doing   work   I   know (I should.)

I
Point to yourself using the right pointer finger.

special
Left hand grabs the pointer finger of the right hand and then pulls it up in front of the chest.

look
The hand makes the letter "V," palm side of the hand toward the body. The hand touches the eyes and then swings back out so the fingers are pointing forward.

me
Point to yourself using the right pointer finger.

I (am)   special.   Look   (at) me.

there
The right pointer is pointing forward in front of the right shoulder and moves forward as if pointing to "there."

like (same as)
Pointer fingers point forward and then move together showing that they are the same.

me
Point to yourself using the right pointer finger.

no one
Right hand makes the letter "O" and moves it from side to side a couple times.

There (is)   no one   (else)   like   me.

SONG 18

Magic Words

Magic Words
(Sung to: "Farmer in the Dell")

What are the magic words?

What are the magic words?

Please, thank-you, excuse me,

and also I'm sorry.

what
The right pointer finger passes over the palm of the left hand.

magic
Hold hands in fists in front of the body and then fling fingers forward making open hands, indicating casting a magic spell.

word
Left hand makes the letter "D" and the right hand makes the letter "G." Then, right pointer finger taps the left pointer finger.

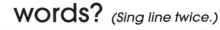

What (are the)   **magic**   **words?** *(Sing line twice.)*

please
The hand is open and flat and moves in a circular motion on the chest.

thank you
The hand, with all four fingers touching the lips, moves forward a few inches.

Please,   **thank-you,**

excuse me
Right hand fingertips brush several times across the left hand palm.

sorry
The fist moves in a circular motion over the heart.

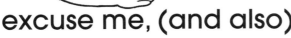

excuse me, (and also)   **I'm sorry.**

SONG 19 Good Table Manners

Good Table Manners
(Sung to: "B-I-N-G-O")

Please sit down its time to eat.
Remember your good manners.
Napkin on your lap.
Chew with a closed mouth.
Say "please" and "thank-you."
And elbows off the table.

please
The hand is open and flat and moves in a circular motion on the chest.

sit
The right pointer and middle fingers are draped over the same two fingers on the left hand. The fingers look like they are sitting.

time
The right pointer finger taps the left wrist several times on the spot where one would wear a watch.

eat
One hand pretends to place food in the mouth.

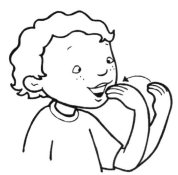

Please   **sit down**   **(its) time**   **(to) eat.**

remember
Pointer finger touches the temple as if trying to remember something.

your
The flat right hand, palm facing out and fingers together, moves forward.

good
The flat hand moves from touching the mouth to being in front of the body, as if something was tasted.

manners
Right hand makes number "5" and then thumb taps the center of chest twice.

Remember   **your**   **good**   **manners.**

napkin
The fingertips wipe over the mouth from side to side twice, as if using a napkin.

on
The right hand moves down and rests "on" the back of the left hand.

your
The flat right hand, palm facing out and fingers together, moves forward.

(Point to lap.)

Napkin   on   your   lap.

chew
Both hands make letter "A." Place right hand on top of left hand and move in small circles - hands moving in opposite directions.

closed mouth
In front of chin, fingertips touch thumb, indicating one should close their mouth.

Chew (with a)   closed mouth.

say
The pointer finger taps the chin twice.

please
The hand is open and flat and moves in a circular motion on the chest.

thank you
The hand, with all four fingers touching the lips, moves forward a few inches.

Say   "please" (and)   "thank-you."

elbow
Tap elbow with the pointer finger.

off
The right hand rests on the back of the left hand. Then the right hand lifts "off" the back of the left hand.

table
The right arm rests on the left arm, as if resting on a table.

(And) elbows   off (the)   table.

SONG 20 Do You Want to Play?

Do You Want to Play?
(Sung to: "Did You Ever See a Lassie?")

(Verse 1) Oh, do you want to play with me?
Play with me? Play with me?
Oh, do you want to play with me?
Let's play with the blocks.
You stack them. Stack higher.
You stack them. Stack higher.
Oh, do you want to play with me?
Let's play with the blocks.

(Verse 2) Oh, do you want to play with me?
Play with me? Play with me?
Oh, do you want to play with me?
Let's play a board game.
It's your turn, then my turn.
It's your turn, then my turn.
Oh, do you want to play with me?
Let's play a board game.

(Verse 3) Oh, do you want to play with me?
Play with me? Play with me?
Oh, do you want to play with me?
Let's play with the ball.
You throw it. I'll catch it.
You throw it. I'll catch it.
Oh, do you want to play with me?
Let's play with the ball.

(Verse 1)

want
Both open hands in front of the body, bring hands back towards chest while fingers bend (as if grabbing).

you
The pointer finger is pointed straight ahead.

play
Both hands make the letter "Y" and twist back and forth at the same time.

me
Point to yourself using the right pointer finger.

(Oh, do)   you   want   (to) play   (with) me?

play
Both hands make the letter "Y" and twist back and forth at the same time.

me
Point to yourself using the right pointer finger.

play
Both hands make the letter "Y" and twist back and forth at the same time.

me
Point to yourself using the right pointer finger.

Play   (with) me?   Play   (with) me?

you
The pointer finger is pointed straight ahead.

want
Both open hands in front of the body, bring hands back towards chest while fingers bend (as if grabbing).

play
Both hands make the letter "Y" and twist back and forth at the same time.

me
Point to yourself using the right pointer finger.

(Oh, do)   you   want   (to) play   (with) me?

let
"L" shaped hands are pointing down and then move to point straight ahead.

play
Both hands make the letter "Y" and twist back and forth at the same time.

block
The right fingertips tap the open left palm above the wrist, and then the left hand fingertips tap the right open palm above the wrist.

  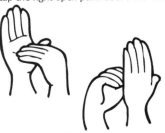

Let's   play (with the)   blocks.

you
The pointer finger is pointed straight ahead.

stack
Alternate moving flat hands up and over each other as if stacking things.

stack
Alternate moving flat hands up and over each other as if stacking things.

higher
Both hands bend fingers and hold them at the shoulders and then move hands up, indicating higher.

You   stack (them).   Stack   higher.

you
The pointer finger is pointed straight ahead.

stack
Alternate moving flat hands up and over each other as if stacking things.

stack
Alternate moving flat hands up and over each other as if stacking things.

higher
Both hands bend fingers and hold them at the shoulders and then move hands up, indicating higher.

You   stack (them).   Stack   higher.

you
The pointer finger is pointed straight ahead.

want
Both open hands in front of the body, bring hands back towards chest while fingers bend (as if grabbing).

play
Both hands make the letter "Y" and twist back and forth at the same time.

me
Point to yourself using the right pointer finger.

(Oh,do)   you   want   (to) play   (with) me?

let
"L" shaped hands are pointing down and then move to point straight ahead.

play
Both hands make the letter "Y" and twist back and forth at the same time.

block
The right fingertips tap the open left palm above the wrist, and then the left hand fingertips tap the right open palm above the wrist.

Let's   play (with the)   blocks.

The bold words are the new lines in verse two. The other sentences remain the same in every verse. Use the signs found on pages 49 & 50.

(Verse 2) Oh, do you want to play with me?
Play with me? Play with me?
Oh, do you want to play with me?
Let's play a board game.
It's your turn, then my turn. It's your turn, then my turn.
Oh, do you want to play with me?
Let's play a board game.

let
"L" shaped hands are pointing down and then move to point straight ahead.

play
Both hands make the letter "Y" and twist back and forth at the same time.

game
Both hands make the letter "A" with the knuckles touching each other and then the thumbs are wiggled.

Let's   play (a)   board game.

your
The flat right hand, palm facing out and fingers together, moves forward.

take turns
Hold the hand in the letter "L" shape in front of the body and then flip it to the side backwards.

my
Place the palm of the right hand flat on the chest.

take turns
Hold the hand in the letter "L" shape in front of the body and then flip it to the side backwards.

(Sing line twice.)

(It's) your   turn.   (Then) my   turn.

let
"L" shaped hands are pointing down and then move to point straight ahead.

play
Both hands make the letter "Y" and twist back and forth at the same time.

game
Both hands make the letter "A" with the knuckles touching each other and then the thumbs are wiggled.

Let's   play (a)   board game.

The bold words are the new lines in verse three. The other sentences remain the same in every verse. Use the signs found on pages 49 & 50.

(Verse 3) Oh, do you want to play with me?
Play with me? Play with me?
Oh, do you want to play with me?
Let's play with the ball.
You throw it. I'll catch it. You throw it. I'll catch it.
Oh, do you want to play with me?
Let's play with the ball.

let
"L" shaped hands are pointing down and then move to point straight ahead.

play
Both hands make the letter "Y" and twist back and forth at the same time.

ball
Both hands are open and the fingertips touch and tap while making the shape of a ball.

Let's

play (with the)

ball.

you
The pointer finger is pointed straight ahead.

throw
Hold the right hand in a fist at the shoulder and then move it forward and fling the fingers open as if throwing something.

I
Point to yourself using the right pointer finger.

catch
Both open hands face forward and pretend to catch.

(Sing line twice.)

You

throw (it.)

I'll

catch (it.)

let
"L" shaped hands are pointing down and then move to point straight ahead.

play
Both hands make the letter "Y" and twist back and forth at the same time.

ball
Both hands are open and the fingertips touch and tap while making the shape of a ball.

Let's

play (with the)

ball.

Little Ponies on the Farm

Little Ponies on the Farm
(Sung to: "She'll Be Coming Round the Mountain")

(Verse 1) There was one little pony on the farm.
There was one little pony on the farm.
She was running all around.
She was jumping up and down.
There was one little pony on the farm.
(Spoken) Here comes another one!

(Verse 2) There were two little ponies on the farm.
There were two little ponies on the farm.
They were running all around.
They were jumping up and down.
There were two little ponies on the farm.

Continue with other verses by simply adding more numbers.
Number signs are found on page 38.

Create additional verses by using other animals.
The signs for "chicken" and "cow" are found on the following page.

(Verses 1–9)

there
The right pointer is pointing forward in front of the right shoulder and moves forward as if pointing to "there."

little
Flat hands move together, indicating that something is little.

pony
Both hands make a "U." Hold them on either side of the head and the fingers wiggle back and forth, just like the ears of a horse.

farm
An open right hand touches the right side of the mouth and then the left side of the mouth.

There (was) (were) **(number sign)** **little** **pony (on the) ponies** **farm.** **(Sing line twice.)**

she
Pointer finger points to the side or to the person.

they
Move the right pointer finger back and forth in front of the body.

run
Each hand looks like a slightly bent letter "L." The pointer finger of one hand pulls on the thumb of the other hand as both hands move forward.

While the hands move forward the extended thumb and pointer finger are wiggled.

around
Move pointer finger, pointing down in a circle around the left pointer finger that is pointing up.

She (was) They (were)

running

(all) around.

---

she
Pointer finger points to the side or to the person.

they
Move the right pointer finger back and forth in front of the body.

jump
The right hand is held in an upside down "V" position and jumps up and down on the palm of the left hand.

up
Pointer finger points up.

down
Pointer finger points down in front of the body.

She (was) They (were)

jumping

up (and)

down.

---

there
The right pointer is pointing forward in front of the right shoulder and moves forward as if pointing to "there."

little
Flat hands move together, indicating that something is little.

pony
Both hands make a "U." Hold them on either side of the head and the fingers wiggle back and forth, just like the ears of a horse.

farm
An open right hand touches the right side of the mouth and then the left side of the mouth.

There (was)/ (number sign) little (were)

pony (on the) ponies

farm.

chicken
Pointer finger and thumb (at lips) open and close like a chicken's beak. Then, the pointer finger scratches for food on left hand palm.

cow
Right hand makes the letter "Y" with the thumb touching the temple then turns back and forth (like horns)

Sign for "chicken."

Sign for "cow."

I'm a Little Monkey

(Songs for Fun: Movement and the Zoo)

I'm a Little Monkey
(Sung to: "I'm a Little Teapot")

I'm a little monkey at the zoo.

Here are my long arms.

Here's my tail, too!

When I get excited I want to play.

Just watch me swing through the trees all day.

I
Point to yourself using the right pointer finger.

little
Flat hands move together, indicating that something is little.

monkey
Fingertips under the arms and scratch armpits (just like a monkey.)

 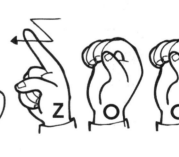

I'm (a)   **little**   **monkey**   **(at the) zoo.**

---

here
Both hands are held palms up and make small circles in front of the chest.

my
Place the palm of the right hand flat on the chest.

long
Right pointer finger touches the left hand wrist and then moves up the arm to the shoulder (showing long).

arm
Put your right fingertips on the bend of your left arm, then move your hand down the arm.

Here (are)   **my**   **long**   **arms.**

---

here
Both hands are held palms up and make small circles in front of the chest.

my
Place the palm of the right hand flat on the chest.

tail
Wiggle the pointer finger like a tail wagging.

Here's   my   tail, (too!)

I
Point to yourself using the right pointer finger.

excited
Both the middle fingers make small circles around both sides of the chest.

I
Point to yourself using the right pointer finger.

want
Both open hands in front of the body, bring hands back towards chest while fingers bend (as if grabbing)..

play
Both hands make the letter "Y" and twist back and forth at the same time.

(When) I   (get) excited   I   want   (to) play.

watch
The hand makes the letter "V," palm side of the hand toward the body. The hand touches the eyes and then swings back out so the fingers are pointing forward.

me
Point to yourself using the right pointer finger.

swing
Both hands make the letter "U" and cross each other and move back and forth as if swinging.

(Just) watch   me   swing

tree
Right elbow rests on the palm of the left hand, and then wiggle the fingers.

all
The hand moves in a circle and then ends up in the palm of the other hand. Shows that everything (all) has been included.

day
Place the left arm parallel to the ground, palm down. Then, with the right hand in a "D" shape, rest the right elbow on the left hand and move the right hand to the left elbow.

(through the) trees   all day.

Phone 911
(Sung to: "Polly Wolly Doodle")

When you need some help, phone 911.
Do you — know what to do?
When you need some help, phone 911.
Police will come help you.

you
The pointer finger is pointed straight ahead. This is a natural gesture for indicating a person.

(When) you

help
The right fist rests in the palm of the left hand, then both hands move up together.

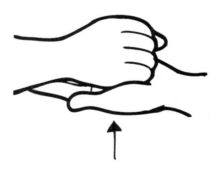

(need some) help,

telephone
The right hand makes the letter "Y". Hold that hand up by the ear as if talking on a phone.

phone

9   1   1.

you
The pointer finger is pointed straight ahead.

know
Fingertips of a flat hand touches the temple.

what
The right pointer finger passes over the palm of the left hand.

(Do) you —   **know**   **what (to do)?**

you
The pointer finger is pointed straight ahead.

help
The right fist rests in the palm of the left hand, then both hands move up together.

(When) you   **(need some) help,**

telephone
The right hand makes the letter "Y". Hold that hand up by the ear as if talking on a phone.

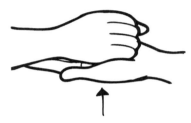

phone   **9**   **1**   **1.**

---

police
Right hand makes the letter "C" and taps it on the chest twice, indicating a police badge.

come
Both pointer fingers beckon, or move towards the body to indicate the concept of come.

help
The right fist rests in the palm of the left hand, then both hands move up together.

you
The pointer finger is pointed straight ahead.

  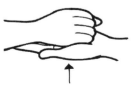 

Police (will)   **come**   **help**   **you.**

SONG 24 Peanut Butter —Jelly

Peanut Butter—Jelly
(Traditional Camp Song)

(Peanut Butter Chant)
Peanut, peanut butter — jelly! Peanut, peanut butter — jelly!

(Verse 1) First you take the peanuts
And you pick 'em and you pick 'em,
And you pick 'em, pick 'em, pick 'em.
Then you smash them and you smash them,
And you smash them, smash them, smash them.
Then you spread it on!   **(repeat chant)**

(Verse 2) Then you take the berries
And you pick 'em and you pick 'em,
And you pick 'em, pick 'em, pick 'em.
Then you smash them and you smash them,
And you smash them, smash them, smash them.
Then you spread it on!   **(repeat chant)**

(Verse 3) Then you take the sandwich
And you bite it and you bite it,
And you bite it, bite it, bite it.
Then you chew it and you chew it,
And you chew it, chew it, chew it.
Then you gulp it and you gulp it,
And you gulp it, gulp it, gulp it.

Repeat chant humming: MmMm, MmMm MmMm—MmMm!
MmMm, MmMm MmMm—MmMm!
Then repeat the peanut butter chant.

(Peanut Butter Chant — Sing line twice.)

peanut
Put the thumb against the back of your front teeth and flick the thumb forward.

peanut butter
Sign "peanut" (thumb against the back of your front teeth and flick the thumb forward). Then, the pointer and middle finger swipes against the left hand palm twice as if spreading peanut butter.

jelly
Right hand makes the letter "J" and then moves the little finger along the palm twice, as if spreading jelly.

Peanut,   peanut butter   — jelly!

(Verse 1)

you
The pointer finger is pointed straight ahead.

take
Both hands make claws in front of the body. Then the hands pull upward into fists, as if "taking" something.

peanut
Put the thumb against the back of your front teeth and flick the thumb forward.

(First) you   take (the)   peanuts,

pick
Thumb and pointer finger are pinched together as the hand moves toward the body, as if picking something.

smash
The palms rub together as if they are smashing something.

pick 'em   smash them

And you pick 'em and you pick 'em,
And you pick 'em, pick 'em, pick 'em.

Then you smash them and you smash them,
And you smash them, smash them, smash them.

you
The pointer finger is pointed straight ahead.

spread
The fingertips on both hands touch each other and then move hands and fingers apart as if spreading.

(Then) you   spread (it on)!

(Verse 2 - is exactly the same as verse 1, except that the word "berries" is substituted for "peanuts." At the end of verse 2, repeat the "Peanut Butter Chant" on page 59.)

berry
The right hand makes an "O" letter shape - then grabs the left little finger and twists it twice.

berries

(Verse 3)

you
The pointer finger is pointed straight ahead.

take
Both hands make claws in front of the body. Then the hands pull upward into fists, as if "taking" something.

sandwich
Hold hands together, palm against palm, and bring fingertips to mouth as if eating a sandwich.

(Then) you　　take (the)　　sandwich,

bite
The right hand makes a claw and grabs the left pointer finger, as if biting the finger.

chew
Both hands makes the letter "A." Place right hand on top of left hand and move in small circles – hands moving in opposite directions.

gulp
Make the hand into the letter "C" shape by the throat and then close the hand into a fist.

bite (it)　　chew (it)　　gulp (it)

And you bite it
and you bite it,
And you bite it,
bite it, bite it.

Then you chew it
and you chew it,
And you chew it,
chew it, chew it.

Then you gulp it
and you gulp it,
And you gulp it,
gulp it, gulp it.

(End the song by humming the Peanut Butter Chant)
MmMm,　MmMm　MmMm — MmMm!
MmMm,　MmMm　MmMm — MmMm!

Then repeat the "Peanut Butter Chant" twice.

peanut
Put the thumb against the back of your front teeth and flick the thumb forward.

peanut butter
Sign "peanut" (thumb against the back of your front teeth and flick the thumb forward). Then, the pointer and middle finger swipes against the left hand palm twice as if spreading peanut butter.

jelly
Right hand makes the letter "J" and then moves the little finger along the palm twice, as if spreading jelly.

Peanut,　peanut butter　— jelly!

SONG 25 It's Raining, It's Pouring

It's Raining, It's Pouring
(Traditional Song)

It's raining, it's pouring.

The old man is snoring.

He bumped his head when he went to bed.

And he couldn't wake up in the morning.

Rain, rain, go away. Come again another day.

rain
Bring both open hands down, and wiggle fingers as if it is raining.

(It's) raining,

pouring
Make sign for rain (bring both open hands down, and wiggle fingers as if it is raining). For pouring do the sign faster and harder.)

(it's) pouring.

old
Make a fist below your chin and pull down as if pulling down a beard.

(The) old

man
With an open hand, use the thumb to touch the forehead and then the chest.

man

snoring
Place right pointer finger under your nose and then pull away with a little bounce as if snoring.

(is) snoring.

bump
The right hand fist bumps into the left palm.

head
Place fingertips on the right temple and then move fingers along the cheek down to the jaw bone.

he
Pointer finger points to the side or to the person.

bed
Rest your head against your cheek.

(He) bumped (his) head (when) he (went to) bed.

he
Pointer finger points to the side or to the person.

not
The right thumb is held under the chin and then pulled forward.

awake
Pinch your pointer fingers and thumbs together next to your eyes, then open them to signal you are awake.

morning
Right arm bends at the elbow with the flat right hand's palm facing the chest. The left hand is placed on the inside of the right bent elbow. The right flat hand then moves like the the sun rising.

(And) he   couldn't   wake up (in the)   morning.

rain
Bring both open hands down, and wiggle fingers as if it is raining.

rain
Bring both open hands down, and wiggle fingers as if it is raining.

go
Both pointer fingers move in an arch and point away from the body.

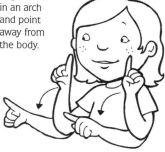

Rain,   rain,   go (away).

come
Both pointer fingers beckon, or move towards the body to indicate the concept of come.

another
Make a "thumbs up" sign and then move the thumb from the left to the right.

day
Place the left arm parallel to the ground, palm down. Then, with the right hand in a "D" shape, rest the right elbow on the left hand and move the right hand to the left elbow.

Come (again)   another   day.

Correlations to the Standards

This book supports the recommended teaching practices outlined in the NAEYC/IRA position statement *Learning to Read and Write: Developmentally Appropriate Practices for Young Children*, the NCTE/IRA Standards for the English Language Arts, NCTM's *Principles and Standards for School Mathematics*, and the National Standards for Arts Education.

NAEYC/IRA Position Statement Learning to Read and Write: Developmentally Appropriate Practices for Young Children

The activities in this book support the following recommended teaching practices for Preschool students:

1. **Adults create positive relationships with children by talking with them, modeling reading and writing, and building children's interest in reading and writing.** *Sing, Sign, & Learn* supports this teaching practice by providing teachers with engaging songs and accompanying signs that build students' interest in literacy.
2. **Teachers provide experiences and materials that help children expand their vocabularies.** Students learn a great deal of new vocabulary related to early childhood and primary themes through the songs in *Sing, Sign, & Learn*

The activities in this book support the following recommended teaching practices for Kindergarten and Primary students:

1. **Teachers provide challenging instruction that expands children's knowledge of their world and expands vocabulary.** Students learn a great deal of new vocabulary related to early childhood and primary themes through the songs in *Sing, Sign, & Learn*.
2. **Teachers adapt teaching strategies based on the individual needs of a child.** The songs in *Sing, Sign, & Learn* support learning through visual, auditory, and kinesthetic routes, enabling teachers to adapt for children with different learning styles.

NCTE/IRA Standards for the English Language Arts

The activities in this book support the following standards:

1. **Students use a variety of strategies to build meaning while reading.** *Sing, Sign, & Learn* supports vocabulary development essential to effective reading.
2. **Students communicate in spoken, written, and visual form, for a variety of purposes and a variety of audiences.** While singing and signing the songs in *Sing, Sign, & Learn*, students communicate orally through singing and visually by making the signs.
3. **Students begin to understand and respect the diversity of language across cultures, regions, ethnicities, and social roles.** *Sing, Sign, & Learn* introduces students to Pidgin Signed English (PSE,) a combination of American Sign Language and English, building their knowledge of another language.
4. **Students become participating members of a variety of literacy communities.** Performing the songs in *Sing, Sign, & Learn* with their students helps teachers build a classroom literacy community.
5. **Students use spoken, written, and visual language for their own purposes, such as to learn, for enjoyment, or to share information.** The songs in *Sing, Sign, & Learn* support students in using spoken and visual language to learn and to have fun.

Principles and Standards for School Mathematics

Selected activities in this book support the following Number and Operations Standards for grades PK-2:

1. **Students count and recognize the number of objects in a set.** The counting/numbers songs in *Sing, Sign, & Learn* support this standard.